Table of Contents

It's a wonderful time when you fall in love and develop special feelings for another person. Each day is something to look forward to when you have that special someone in your life. When you're in a relationship, it's important to keep trying to improve on the special gifts that each day will bring for you.

You'll find lots of great quotes, discussions, and tips in this guide that will allow you to strengthen your love relationship. *Each time you put forth an effort you'll be encouraging your love to grow even more.*

The quotes in the guide are all from famous people and their thoughts on strengthening love. Followed is a discussion that will give you more information on how to understand the quotes.

As you progress through the guide, pay special attention to the Self Reflection Questions. They are there to help you to

think about what you're doing
in your current relationship.
Use them to reflect on the
different points that they bring
up to assist you in
understanding your
relationship even better.

It's your relationship. *Do
everything you can to
strengthen your love with the
tips ahead.*

Falling in Love

Eleanor Roosevelt's quote is indicative of how human we all are. A new relationship is always kind of scary – exciting, but scary at the same time. It's natural to feel a bit uncomfortable when you're falling in love.

Developing confidence in your budding relationship will lessen your fears. Remember that building a relationship takes time. Instead of wondering how much your new friend cares about you, *switch your focus to getting to know each other.* Learn their likes and dislikes. Discover their passions and how they feel about important issues. Share your hopes and dreams together.

The relationship will naturally progress as you learn more about each other and you won't be left wondering how they feel.

Self-Reflection Questions:

1. Do you take love for granted? How can you show your appreciation for even the little things that your new love does for you?

2. Are you guarded when falling in love? How can you be more open about your feelings?

3. What are some ways you can get to know each other better?

Friendship in Love

With Lord Byron's quote, we find that friendships do turn into love relationships. In fact, new studies show that married couples are happier, and enjoy a more enduring love, when they consider their spouse to be their best friend as well as their lover.

You can strengthen your love just by becoming better friends!

On the other hand, though, it's difficult to become only friends once you've loved someone in a romantic relationship. This challenge is important to keep in mind if you wish to pursue a romantic relationship with a good friend. If things do go awry, you could lose that friend.

Self-Reflection Questions:

1. Are you in a love relationship that started as a friendship?

2. Have you ever wanted to return to being "just friends" after being romantically

involved? How did it work
out?

3. What can you do to become
a better friend to your lover?

Destiny in Love

Julia Roberts' take on love is very ingenious. She believes that two people that are destined to be together will fall in love regardless of the circumstances. This is a very simplistic look at love that allows someone to look for someone that they're truly able to bond with.

Have you met someone that you feel connected with right from the start? You might have found your soul mate and are destined to be together.

When you feel as if you've known someone forever, it will be easy for you to get along with them. It will come naturally. This will allow you and your loved one to develop deep feelings quickly.

Self-Reflection Questions:

1. Do you feel like you're in a destined relationship?

2. Will you look for a partner
   that also feels destined to be
   with you?

3. How can you tell if you're
   destined to be together?

Nurture Love

John Lennon believes that love needs to be worked at, and he sees it as something that needs to be nurtured. *Your love will continue to grow as long as it's treated with the importance it deserves.*

Try these tips to nurture your love:

- Say that you love the person often.
- Do something nice for them on a daily basis.
- Talk openly and honestly with your loved one.
- Spend time together on a regular basis.

Loving someone takes time.
During the process, you'll
enjoy getting to know them
and helping your relationship
grow.

Self-Reflection Questions:

1. How do you nurture your
   relationship?

2. Do you find it easy to be in
   love with someone else?
   Why or why not?

3. Can you force someone to
   fall in love with you?

Windows to the Soul

This Victor Hugo quote gives a man some insight on understanding women. When you love completely, you'll notice many nuances about the one you love. *You'll be fulfilled in a variety of ways, not just verbally.*

Noticing the special qualities about your loved one is very important. Watch for nonverbal clues for more complete communication.

- Notice the body language of your partner.

- Understand their emotions.
- Listen to your partner intently.

Always show love in a personal and physical way to enhance your love relationship. Hug and hold hands as often as possible.

Self-Reflection Questions:

1. How can you understand your partner more completely?

2. Can love be spoken without words?

3. Is it important to communicate nonverbally when a couple is in love?

Love is Intense

When you're in love, you'll have a variety of feelings that will be intense. Everything that you get to know about the

other person will mean
something to you.

*Mother Teresa believes that
love is intense, yet it doesn't
need to be demanding
because it's a giving process.*

When you care about
someone, it's wonderful to
give freely to them without
wanting something in return.

Self-Reflection Questions:

1. Do you feel that your love is intense? Why or why not?

2. When do you give freely in your love relationship?

3. How can you give more to the relationship to make it stronger?

Beginnings of Love

"The beginning of love is to let those we love be perfectly themselves, and not to twist them to our own image."
-Thomas Merton

When you fall in love with someone, it's important to accept them as they are – to know that they have both wonderful traits and also some not-so-pleasing qualities, but this is one you love - without

thinking that you'll just change
them down the road.

Knowing that you accept them
just as they are will help them
feel comfortable with you.
They can be more open as you
share feelings, hopes, and
dreams together. This
acceptance and sharing will
bring you closer and closer
together.

Make them feel special
whenever you are together so
that they know that they are
loved.

Be attentive to their needs. When they are feeling comfortable enough to open up, they will begin to love freely.

Self-Reflection Questions:

1. How can you and your partner get to know each other better?

2. Are you open to accepting the person you love just as they are?

3. Do you let your partner have their own wants and needs in addition to your goals as a couple?

Sharing Your Life

Will Smith sums it up nicely by saying it is time to *share your life when you are happy with it.* Since there is so much to share when you are happy, another person will gravitate to you. Making your life the best it can be is important when you want to attract a loving partner. They can tell when you're happy.

Try these actions to remind you of how much you enjoy your life:

- Smile a lot.
- Reflect on how much you've accomplished in your life.

- Feel grateful for your blessings.
- Enjoy each day.

When you're happy with your life, you will show it to others and they will want to get to know you. You'll attract a lovely person into your life.

Self-Reflection Questions:

1. Are you happy with the things that you've done in your life?

2. How can you make room in your life for someone to love?

3. When is a quiet moment in your day when you can reflect on your blessings?

Love Goes Beyond Friendship

"Love is friendship that has caught fire. It is quiet understanding, mutual confidence, sharing and forgiving. It is loyalty through

good and bad times. It settles for less than perfection and makes allowances for human weaknesses".
-Ann Landers

Ann Landers believes that love encompasses many different aspects of the human personality. She sees that *there are many reasons why people fall in love with one another*.

By being a loving person, you will attract love yourself. There are so many ways that you can show love to the one you adore.

Self-Reflection Questions:

1. How has your friendship with your partner caught fire?

2. What are some ways in which you show loyalty to your partner?

3. How can you remind
   yourself to make allowances
   for their imperfections?

Staying Close in Love

"The best thing to hold onto is each other."
–Audrey Hepburn

When Audrey Hepburn talks about love, she wants people to understand how much they mean to each other and realize how they will always be there for each other no matter what happens.

When you're in love, you and your lover are happier together than you are apart, and you show this in your everyday lives.

Having the ability to be close to another human being is a blessing. When you find someone that you love, hold on to them. Show them that you love them in both good times and bad. Knowing that you can count on each other's love regardless of your circumstances will give you both added confidence in the strength of your relationship.

Self-Reflection Questions:

1. How do you show your commitment to your love?

2. How can you demonstrate your love when times are good?

3. How can you demonstrate your love when your circumstances are challenging?

Love Is Gentle

"A gentle heart is tied with an easy thread."
–George Herbert

In his quote, George Herbert reflects on how fragile a love

relationship is and that it needs gentle care to survive.

What are ways that you can take gentle care of your loving relationship?

Try these techniques:

- Listen when your partner has something to say and be responsive.

- Be positive. Look forward to your life together each day.
- Always remember that you love them, even when you disagree on something.
- Give your lover sincere compliments.
- Say "I love you" in both your words and actions.

Self-Reflection Questions:

1. How would you describe your tone of voice when speaking to your partner?

2. What do you say when
   talking about your partner?
   Are you focusing on
   negative or positive aspects
   of the one you love?

3. What are some new ways you can show your love?

Closest Friends

"The relationship between husband and wife is one of closest friends."
-B. R. Ambedkar

When you fall in love, are you open to developing the relationship further? Having a future with someone is important, and you'll want to be able to make a commitment to them. Becoming a man and a wife is the highest form of commitment.

Being friends with your mate enhances your relationship. *Do things together and share common interests.*

Finding time to care is important. Consider these ideas to free up time to be together:

- Schedule days or nights that you can spend time alone together.
- Keep your romance growing.

- Be supportive of your loved one when they need to be comforted.
- Be pleasant, courteous, and cooperative.
- Understand your partner's needs.

Self-Reflection Questions:

1. Are you the closest friends with your mate?

2. How often do you spend time alone together?

3. How can you encourage more open communication with your loved one?

Deep Love

*"Being deeply loved by someone gives you strength,
while loving someone deeply gives you courage."*
-Lao Tzu

In Lao Tzu's quote, you'll see that *the strength comes from within you when you are in a loving relationship.* You'll feel empowered to show how much you care.

Courage will come naturally when you fall in love. In many ways, you'll feel like you never felt before in your life. It will give you the courage to take on other achievements that you never thought you could do before.

Self-Reflection Questions:

1. How has your love given you courage?

2. Consider some ways in
   which your relationship
   makes you feel stronger.

3. Do you feel that you can
   deepen your love? How?

Making Loving Connection

"The more connections you make with your lover, not just between your bodies, but between your minds, your hearts and your souls, the more you will strengthen the

*fabric of your relationship,
and the more real moments
you will experience together."
-Barbara de Angelis*

Barbara de Angelis understands that a love relationship entails an effort on both parts that includes connections between the mind, heart, soul, and body.

Try these techniques to strengthen your ties:

- Speak openly and honestly about your true feelings.

- Listen intently to what your partner is saying about their wants and needs.
- Actively participate in your partnership on all levels.

Give freely and honestly to allow your partner to feel comfortable in sharing their life with you.

Self-Reflection Questions:

1. How can you connect with
   your partner in mind, heart,
   and soul, not just body?

2. What are some new ways
   you can strengthen the fabric
   of your relationship?

3. Have you ever felt like you
   were experiencing a perfect
   moment with your partner?
   When?

Conclusion

Strengthening your love
relationship is very important.
You'll find that it will be worth
the effort to have that special
someone in your life to share
all the ups and downs with.
When you put a lot into the
relationship, it will result in
many happy moments
together.

When you reflect on love,
you'll be able to deepen the
feelings in your relationship
tremendously. You'll be able

to strengthen the ties between you and your loved one.

Love is an ongoing process, one that takes nurturing and caring. When you find the person that is right for you, it will come easily to show them how much you care. With so many wonderful things to enjoy when you're in love, you'll want to make the very most of the time that you spend with your special someone.

Working on your love relationship will bring you many benefits. *Love is worth the effort.* Enjoy!

Next, we will complete a few worksheets to delve deeper, to better assist you.

#1 Barriers to Communication Assessment

Answer yes or no to the following. Do you generally:

___ Assume you understand without clarifying?

___ Jump to conclusions before getting the facts?

___ Criticize instead of complaining?

___ Shut down emotionally and/or shut out your partner?

___ Bring up old stuff from the past? ___ Yell, name-call, slam doors, etc.?

___ Pull other people into arguments?

___ Blame - "It's all your fault!"?

___ *Shame - "How could you?"*

___ *Preach - "You should…"?*

___ *Zone Out – ignoring or distracting with tv, computers, phones?*

___ *Refuse to talk about it*

___ *Minimize – "It's not a big deal – you're overreacting."*

___ *Dramatize – becoming overly emotional or melodramatic*

___ *Label – "You're a sociopath!" or "Don't be so neurotic!"*

Check Scores:

SCORES

Count the number of 'yes' responses to see how well you communicate.

0-5 – You are doing pretty well, but may need some help – let's talk about this.

6-10 – You may be headed for trouble – we need to talk soon.

11 and over – You are in the danger zone – let's talk ASAP.

#2 Family Patterns Assessment

Check all that apply to you.

___ **My parents communicated openly and honestly.**

___ **My parents showed affection to each other.**

___ **My parents said 'I love you' to each other often.**

___ **My parents handled conflict peacefully and effectively – did not let it slide.**

____ My parents were in agreement on how to manage the finances.

____ My parents had specific roles in managing the household chores and it worked.

____ My parents did not have physical fights or hurt each other.

____ When my parents argued, they did so privately.

____ My parents maintained other healthy friendships outside the marriage.

____ My parents taught me how to have a healthy relationship and family.

Bring this to your session so we can discuss your responses.

#3 Healthy Boundaries Assessment

Respond to the following with:
1-Rarely
2-Sometimes
3-Frequently

____ I ask for what I want/need directly.

____ I let people know when they are being unreasonable or demanding.

____ I say 'no' without feeling obligated or guilty.

____ I set limits on my time, resources and availability.

____ I have a healthy sense of interdependence – not too dependent or independent.

____ I generally take care of my needs before trying to help others.

____ People respect my limits.

___ *I do not over-commit myself.*

___ *I do not reinforce behavior that I dislike by passively condoning it.*

___ *People do not take me for granted.*

Scoring:

Review your responses and consider the following for each statement.

1 – Rarely – Needs improvement - let's talk about how to strengthen this area.

2 – Sometimes – Good job! We can come up with ideas to help you be more consistent.

3 – Frequently – Great job! Keep up the good work!

As we reach the end of this journey together, I hope that the insights and knowledge shared in this book have been enlightening and beneficial to you. It has been my pleasure to share my experiences and expertise with you.

If you found the content of this book valuable and wish to delve deeper into the subject, I offer a range of services that might interest you. These include personal coaching, workshops, and online courses, all designed to help you further develop your skills and understanding.

For more information about these services, please visit my website at www.wyshinawest.com.

You can also reach out to me directly at: askcoachshina@gmail.com for any inquiries or to discuss how we can work together to achieve your goals.

Thank you once again for joining me on this journey. I look forward to working with you in the near future.

www.ingramcontent.com/pod-product-compliance
Lightning Source LLC
Chambersburg PA
CBHW081953160726
47999CB00008B/2608